Gulla

Africa's Seed in th

Volume I

St. Helena Serenity

written by Queen Quet Marquetta L. Goodwine

www.QueenQuet.com

To Sisters Diane & Danielle and Brother Bill:

May serenity forever fill your soul.

Peace,
Queen Quet
6/25/16

© 2009 Second Edition by Queen Quet Marquetta L. Goodwine

© 1995 Marquetta L. Goodwine

Go to www.gullahgeechee.biz to obtain additional copies of this book and the additional volumes of this series:

Volume II *Gawd Dun Smile Pun Wi: Beaufort Isles*

Volume III *Frum Wi Soul ta de Soil: Cotton, Rice, and Indigo*

Volume IV *365-366*

Volume V *Chas'tun an e Islandts*

Contact the *Gullah/Geechee Sea Island Coalition*

Post Office Box 1207

St. Helena Island SC 29920

(843) 838-1171

GullGeeCo@aol.com

www.gullahgeechee.net

Also available are *"Tinkin' 'bout Famlee: A Geechee Doung Novella"*

and *"Brother and Sister...Heart to Heart"* by Marquetta L. and Ronald Goodwine.

and the activity book, *"Wi Tings: Gullah/Geechee Living Traditions"*

***

"As I look out over the creek filled with marsh toward Edding Landing on St. Helena Island, SC, the spirits of my ancestors speak to me from their nearby resting place. I can hear and feel them sing and I am a vessel for their words..."

• Queen Quet Marquetta L. Goodwine

© 2009 Photos by Kumar L. Goodwine-Kennedy and Queen Quet

Table of Contents

Preface
Dedication
Introduction
St. Helena's Song
Sing to the Spirit
With the Power
Journey On...
Epilogue
Bibliography

Preface

This is Volume I of a series about the Gullah/Geechee cultures of the Sea Islands within the Gullah/Geechee Nation. It is estimated that there are at least 2000 islands in the string of islands in the Atlantic Ocean along the coast of the United States from North Carolina to Florida. Many of these are uninhabitable, but the others were the fertile soil from whence grew the Gullah/Geechee culture and strong proud Africans in America.

Each volume in the series will explain a different aspect of the rich African cultures that came together in to the Gullah/Geechee Nation. This volume focuses on the extraordinary history of St. Helena Island in Beaufort County, SC. St. Helena is one the last of the mid-size islands that has a contiguous Gullah/Geechee community throughout the entire island.

St. Helena Island is located midway between Charleston, South Carolina and Savannah, Georgia and is the crown jewel of "beautiful Beaufort by the sea." This is your opportunity to journey to St. Helena in spirit and I am sure that just like many others that have learned about us, "hunnuh ga wan cum fa see."

Dedication

When Primus Holmes began his life journey I am sure that he did not know that he would be the founding father of a strong Sea Island Gullah/Geechee family. This family withstood chattel enslavement, Reconstruction, Jim Crow, the Civil Rights era, and the dawn of the space age. I am sure that he did not know that his descendent, Henry, who was known as "Wikky" would meet Rita, the daughter of Eliza and Toby, and bring forth:

Benjamin

Albertha

Carolee

Ardel

Ruth

Rebecca

Nellie

Andrew

and their many other children.

I dedicate this book to all of Primus and Eliza and Toby's ancestors and their descendants. This is in tribute to the nurturing educating relationship that Carolee had with their father, Wikky. She has taken the time to pass on the stories, the respect, the heritage, and the pride that was instilled in her and she tempered it with love.

So, Rita, Wikky, and Carolee, these words are for you. Thank you for life, love, knowledge, and the blessings of being a "Gullah/Geechee gal."

For all those who read this:

I hope that as you open this Sea Island treasure chest, you will find a jewel that you will lock in your heart...

Introduction

"In the beginning, God created the heavens and the earth." The earth was later populated and enriched with the seeds of "Alkebulan" which we now call "Africa." As these seeds were nurtured by the Spirit, they grew to develop rich societies throughout the continent. Although gold, brass, silver, gemstones, and cowry shells were and are in abundance in Africa, these cultures were rich because of the knowledge, wisdom, and spiritual balance that the people used in their relationships with other entities in the universe other people, vegetation, earth, water, gems, and other minerals.

Many Africans lived on the west coast of the continent (even though they had connections to other areas especially the extraordinary kingdom of Kemet (Egypt)). As they went out to sea to fish and trade; as they harvested rice and other crops; as they cooked, sewed baskets, sang songs, and told stories, they did not anticipate this lifestyle coming to an end, but others came in and disrupted things.

As "European conquest" began to run rampant throughout Alkebulan, the invaders got knowledge of these industrious people on the west coast. The invaders entered these lands and killed and kidnapped, raped, and plundered. These people who were living as one with the universe and were in tune with the Creator would not simply stand by and see their families destroyed. So, "the war was on!"

The invaders entered places that we now call Ghana, Senegal, the Ivory Coast, Angola, Gambia, Liberia, and Sierra Leone and took "prisoners of this war" (which were the enslaved Africans that we were taught to call "slaves"). The captured parties were forced through the "doors of no return" into the bellies of the ships which set sail across the Middle Passage.

The trip was one of sheer terror with people separated from members of their families and from others that spoke their native tongues. People were shackled to others that were weeping, wailing, and calling out to God and the ancestors. Due to the stench and unsanitary conditions caused by urine, defecation, vomit and dead bodies that also occupied extremely small spaces in which those that were strong enough to remain alive were shackled, many got ill. Some simply died from broken hearts as they thought of the mass murders of their families that they had witnessed on the shore.

With human cargo in tow, these ships journeyed toward the "New World." Many African captives held strong to their sanity and fought this inhumane treatment! The battles in this war continued as people would manage to break their chains and take over ships. Some ships were successfully taken from their crews and turned back toward the continent. Who knows it any made it back to their homeland? Some did dock at the shores of what are now the Caribbean islands and the shores of the "New World" where they had to fight in court for the freedom that was rightfully theirs.

Millions didn't make it through the battles. Some even chose death over enslavement. For the ones that did make it through the first leg of the journey, some of them were traded for sugar, molasses, rum, and other items in Jamaica, Cape Verde, Barbados, the Bahamas, Hispanola, etc. These were the points that connected to make the first side of the TransAtlantic "slave trade triangle."

The ships now loaded with human, edible and material cargo set sail on the second side of the triangle to the "New World"-America. Many of those that came from Angola and the Windward Coast in the area of Sierra Leone, had been left in Barbados, but the ships continued on their journeys and dropped the rest of these rich human seeds on the soil of "Chicora" which was renamed the "Carolinas." As these seeds blossomed during this period of land usurping by Europeans from indigenous people, seeds were blown from the Carolinas, to Georgia, and Florida (a few even settled in the deltas of the "deep south").

The seeds flourished on isolated islands in the Atlantic Ocean that we now call the Sea Islands. The Africans that grew from these seeds bore a rich, sweet, powerful fruit with a spiritual covering. These fruits are what we now call "Gullah" and "Geechee."

One of the counties of South Carolina's that is actually a string of islands is Beaufort. The branches of the family tree of the native Gullah/Geechee islanders include Bajan, Sierra Leonean, Senegalese, Madagascaran, Cusabo, Yamassee, Cherokee, Creek, and many others. The natives of St. Helena Island in Beaufort are a wonderful representation at the preservation of African culture in America.

St. Helena's natives are the legacy of the warriors (both male and female) that fought their way from Africa and built a spiritual kingdom in a foreign land. This Sea Island community is still held together by communal ties. Islanders know "emptee sak cyan stand upright 'lone." Therefore, everyone works to hold up the sides of the community as it is filled with stories, songs, love, and communal spirit.

Thank you for joining the journey to the Sea Isles of the Gullah/Geechee Nation. I hope that you will feel the "serenity of St. Helena."

• Queen Quet Marquetta L. Goodwine

St. Helena's Song

I bin da tink bout wha mama sey

Win dey clen e ga be a new dey.

I tink bout how de old folk sey,

"Trubull ain gwine lass always."

Hold fast to the spirit and fight fa de tru ting.

Lift ya spirit and ya voice and le dem sing.

In the 1520s a ship from Spain traveled up the marsh strewn coast of the Atlantic and the crew breathed in the clean salt filled air. As Francisco Gordillo looked out over the land and sea, his eyes captured a scene of beauty. This reminded him of a saint, Santa Elena, so he decided to name this place in her honor-"Punta de Santa Elena." This area went from Edisto, South Carolina to Savannah, Georgia and was surrounded by St. Helena's Sound, the Combahee River, the Savannah River, and the Atlantic Ocean.

The native people of the area are called "Escamacu." They were among the 18 independent tribes of the "Cusabo." The Escamacu War took place from 1576 to 1579. During this time, the Edisto moved north to the area of the island that today bears their name. In 1565 the Escamacu began occupying the land between the Broad and Savannah Rivers. However, after the war, they moved north to begin occupying St. Helena Island. The Queen of Saint Helena Island ceded the lands bounded to the north or east by the Ashepoo, Edisto, and uninhabited lands and to the southwest by the Kussah, Wimbee, and uninhabited lands to them. Within 100 years, the numbers of the indigenous people occupying the area were greatly reduced. This came simultaneously with the arrival of Spanish and European "settlers."

Spain tried to settle Port Royal, which is west of St. Helena, many times between 1521 and 1566. The first settlement that they had was located along the Waccamaw River. In 1566 Jean Ribaut and the French Hugenots built a fort on St. Helena Island not far from where they started a colony in Port Royal in 1562. They eventually abandoned both of these. The indigenous or Native Americans did not make it easy for any for any of these people to come in and stake claims for their queens and kings.

On 24 March 1663, a charter was granted by the king of England for the settlement of what is now Carolina. This charter opened new doors for British Loyalists who had been in Barbados to have new plots of land on which to build homes and gain wealth. The first expedition to the area was conducted by Captain William Hilton. His name is still synonymous with wealth in the Sea Islands given that fact that Hilton Head Island bears his name.

Captain William Hilton sailed out of Speightstown in Barbados on August 10, 1663 in order to find a suitable location for a settlement for the English crown. In 16 days, Hilton arrived near "St. Ellens" where he was met by a group of the indigenous Americans or Native Americans who held many of his crew members hostage. Hilton wrote of the ruins of an old fort that they saw located at the site. Archeologists believe that the meeting that he had at a round house that was made of Palmetto leaves was the "Indian Council House" on St. Helena. St. Helena still bears the sacred "Indian mound" for which an area of the island is named "Indian Hill." However, this is not the location of the council house.

The years that followed brought many disasters to the men that attempted to journey across the Atlantic to Barbados through the Bahamas to their final destination in the Carolinas. After the destruction of numerous ships, and the capture, death of crews, and battles with indigenous people, November 1, 1670 finally was the date of the settlement of Charles Towne at Albemarle Point by Lord Ashley. This area is now Charleston which is on the Ashley River.

Indigenous people supplied them with fish and game for minimal sums. They even assisted them in clearing and cultivating the land. As the British Lords Proprietors came to the Carolinas in 1671 and 1672, they also brought their servants and enslaved Africans.

Early on in Carolina's history, "before 1710, African slaves began to outnumber white inhabitants, by mid-century, there were roughly twice as many Africans as whites and the trend continued." As the population expanded, Caucasian settlers sought more property. In 1698, Thomas Naire who was employed by the General Assembly of South Carolina as an Indian agent received a warrant to take out land on St. Helena. Many more were to follow.

The tracts of land that were originally taken out by warrants were eventually sold and settled on. To this day, St. Helena bears the names of the plantation owners that bought tracts of land. These include Capers, Fripp, (as is the case with plantations including Ann Fripp, Tom Fripp, and John Fripp), Eddings, Chaplin, Jenkins, Scott, Coffins Point, McTuereous, Pritchard, Dr. and Edding White, Wallace, Fuller, and Croft.

Before these men were able to obtain "ownership" of the land, the original residents had to be removed as far as they were concerned. Despite the fact that local native people had helped that European newcomers with cultivating gardens and fields, traded fish and game with them and taught the how to navigate the inland waterways, the Europeans began seeing the natives as a problem because they could not expand their "settlements" with the "Indians" here.

As time went on, the native people, especially the Yamassees, continued to trade with the Europeans which led to economic weakness for them. The Yamassee had found a "market" for themselves by being involved in "slave raiding." This ethnic group migrated from the South Carolina-Georgia boarder into Florida and back. They took up residence along the South Carolina coast by 1685 and from there became known as the principal agents in the Indian slave trade until the 1715 Yamassee War. They ended up going to many of the missions in the St. Augustine, Florida area. Just as many of the Gullah/Geechees did, many Yamassees ended up going into Cuba and Mexico in the latter 1700s.

Prior to their departure westward, many of the native peoples developed a taste for rum which led to the weakening of their forces and communities. This was a direct benefit to the Europeans that had set their sites on this area that was slowly becoming known as "the Carolinas."   According to Theodore Rosengarten:

> "the provincial government set aside a reservation of land in 1707 for ten Yamassee towns-the first Indian reservation in America.
>
> Whites observed the boundaries for a few years, infrequent   violations involved mainly incursions of cattle onto Indian land. In 1711, the English ordered a highway built from the Edisto River to Port Royal and St. Helena Islands, and the Lords Proprietors described plans for a seaport on Port Royal to be called Beaufort Town. The creation of an administrative division called St. Helena Parish was announced in 1712."

After feeling the effects of this overwhelming betrayal, the Yamassee decided to finally fight back. On April 11, 1715, they joined forces with the Creek and killed the white traders in their territories. Attacks followed against white settlements on a 120-mile front from the Savannah to the Santee River.

Most historians seem to credit Creeks for strategizing attacks such as this. Since the Creeks stayed in their secluded areas (generally hills) the turmoil only benefitted them. Refugees often became members of their population and their prosperity was increased with the spread of European trade.

The destruction of the Yamassees was only the beginning of the elimination of the indigenous people in the region. "The Creeks waxed stronger, and the Carolina colonies grew in wealth and colonists. By the 1730s upward of 200 ships a year left Charleston laden with the merchandise of the growth of the country." "By 1740 the once plentiful coastal peoples had disappeared."

Even though the Europeans thought that they had eliminated the "Indians," they had not completely disappeared. In fact, many of them that had been captured were enslaved with and became part of African families. The destruction of the heritage and family ties of

these people was not a concern of the Europeans who were seeking new lives of their own.

With greed in heart and the potential of wealth on their minds, a faction of settlers were able to remove the Lords Proprietors from their position of leadership. Thus, the doors to the islands were opened and in moved the Europeans with the Africans that they were enslaving and their Anglo indentured servants.

All of these people that settled the Carolinas needed laborers to build their homes, cultivate their crops, and cater to their families. As a result "slave ports" were set up on the western coast of Africa and the business of "slave trading" became the order of the day. By 1750, Bunce Island in the Sierra Leone River was a "slave shipyard."

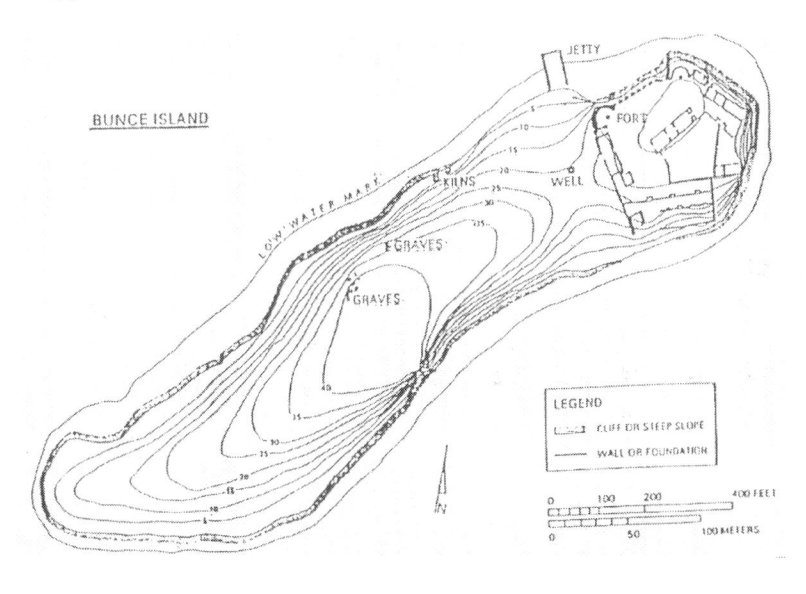

"Slave castles" and "slave forts" also existed in Ghana and Senegal. Many of those who were bought and sold at these locations were brought to the Sea Islands of Charleston, Beaufort and the surrounding areas.

The enslaved Africans that were on St. Helena and neighboring islands built these islands, and formed and maintained the rich Gullah/Geechee culture. There have been hundreds of people that have and still continue to study Gullah/Geechee people because they are amazed at the "Africanisms" that remains a part of their lives. Although it is a unique occurrence given the devastation and destruction that slavery had upon African families, it obviously was not impossible.

The enslaved Africans that are the ancestors of today's native Gullah/Geechees were put on the islands with one another and an overseer. As the years went on, the "massas" began to trust a few "nigras" to become overseers of their own people. These Negroes were called "drivers."

The plantation owners lived on the mainland in the townships which are now cities such as Beaufort. They did not stay on the island for many reasons:

> • Mosquitoes are more abundant near the marshes and many enslaved Africans developed immunity to the bites of these insects that carried such diseases as

malaria. However, the Anglo people were not immune and many died from sicknesses associated with the bites when many Africans would only suffer slight illness.

- The isolation of the islands was simply to insure productivity of the Africans. So, as they worked there, the owners were off making other business deals and their wives were being catered to by other servants and enslaved people on their estates.

- Myths that Africans turned into animals at night were believed by many Anglo people for decades.

- "Voodoo" was not recognized as a religion by Anglo people. It was (and still is) seen as something mystical and something to be feared.

The owners would periodically get in their boats and come and check on their "slaves" and their crops which included okra, corn, green beans, peas, tomatoes, potatoes, watermelons, squash, indigo, rice, and cotton. The latter three made rich men out of many settlers even though it was African technology and agriculture that made these prosper. Many of these crops were already a part of the lives of Africans in Alkebulan. So, they continued to transfer their knowledge into New World soil in order to have these things prosper.

Rice was successfully introduced on the mainland in 1700. It is believed that the "Carolina Gold" seeds came from Madagascar. "Quickly large estates were enclosed and shiploads of slaves were removed to Carolina," according to Rosengarten. No doubt some of these captives were placed on the Sea Islands including St. Helena to work this crop that would become one of the three crops that would help build the infrastructure of the new country.

Rice was grown well into the early 1900s, but was given up thereafter due to the changes in the land (which needs to be low and extremely moist) and the extensiveness of preparation for cooking it. According to Carolee Holmes Brown, her family used to "take all the furniture outside." Then everybody would beat the stalks until the rice would fall off. After this the rice would need to be separated from the husk. The separation process used on the Sea Islands was the same that was done on the Windward Coast for decades.

The rice would be put into a pan or a flat basket called a "fanna." The fanna is lifted up and down in the air as if flipping pancakes. The wind then helps the separation process by blowing husk out and leaving the rice to land in the fanna.

Rice has been and still is used in the Sea Islands on a daily basis. It can be eaten as a breakfast cereal (if someone doesn't have or want to eat grits) and may come with lunch. However, it almost always comes with a true Sea Island Gullah/Geechee dinner in the form of red rice, hoppin John, or just a bed for gumbo and gravy.

Unlike rice, indigo which is a blue dye (still used in many west African countries to die cloths) is currently not often found in the Sea Islands. Over the years using indigo, it begins to dye the skin. If someone were to stop working in it long enough, their skin may return to its normal color. However, there are some cases that indicated poisoning from working in the dye. This is no doubt from the agents that were used to extract the dye from the plant.

Of all the island crops, Sea Island cotton brought in the most income. This cotton was very fine and long. Thus, it became the most expensive cotton on the market. It also took extensive work to grow in comparison to upland cotton and the cotton grown in the "deep south." The production of a crop took eighteen months.

The three aforementioned crops were sold at markets along with various vegetables and fruits. Sometimes enslaved Africans that were "field hands" were allowed to utilize plots of land on which to cultivate their own crops. They still could not do whatever they wanted with what they grew however. In fact, "A statute from 1751 prohibited slaves from selling corn to anyone, but their master..."

In addition to crop cultivation, raising hogs continues to be a part of Sea Island life. Pork has and continues to be a portion of the Sea Island diet. Hogs are generally raised for profit. Just as people raise hogs now and take them to the market when the prices are high, "pigs provided the major cash income for slaves; the money was used to buy sugar, coffee, wheat flour, tobacco, and other small luxuries."

The raising of crops, livestock (which includes chickens, ducks, turkeys, geese, cows, and pigs which are all still raised on the islands currently), and families required land. White men who were not currently indentured servants were usually able to obtain land through a "headright" which was "an allotment of land based on the number of people in his household, including servants and slaves." Rosengarten detailed what this amounted to in 1670:

"...the headright for a free white man was 150 acres, this was reduced in 1672 to 100 acres and in 1682 to 50 acres. Each Negro man brought his owner 20 acres in 1670, and each Negro woman brought 10."

Numerous accounts of the chattel slavery system (which the British developed and fully exploited) seem to agree that even though Anglo and Native Americans were used for the hard labor, field work, clearing of land, and building of buildings required, Africans were preferred because they worked harder and were not prone to certain methods of resistance such as starving themselves to death. In fact, many of those that were "slavers" recount quotes such as "It was easier to discipline Africans, to force them to accept the frightful labor and meager rewards..."

Some Africans allowed themselves to be converted to "Negroes" in order to so-called "take advantage" of some of these meager rewards (which often only amounted to a horse and buggy, a shack to live in, and/or some of 'massas' hand me downs) and became "drivers." The role of the overseers and drivers was not just to see that work got done. They were also to make sure that the enslaved Africans did not escape.

A driver was one the most contemptible people in the slavery system because he often looked just like and came from the bloodline and womb of the people he now whipped and/or told on. The way in which drivers were seen by those being "driven" was captured in *Army Life in a Black Regiment* by Thomas Wentworth Higginson:

The Driver

"O, de ole nigger-driver!

O, gwine away!

Fust ting my mammy tell me,

O, gwine away!

Tell me 'bout de nigger-driver,

O, gwine away!

Nigger-driver second devil,

O gwine away!

Best ting for do he driver,

O gwine away!

Knock he down and spoil the labor,

O gwine away!

I am sure that many herbs could have been given to these drivers to make them go away, but instead this dream to go away was often fulfilled by the enslaved African. This individual would not only "go away" from the driver, but the plantation itself. Strong alliances formed between a number of indigenous Americans and the enslaved Africans. These alliances helped many of the captives escape bondage and set off on the "road to freedom."

Many people quietly eased away from the fields into the woods and navigated the waterways to other islands. Some even went to the mainland eventually and made their way north, south, east, and west.

Wherever these "maroons" built their new communities, they spread the Gullah/Geechee seed a little further.

Some of these seeds made their way to Florida which was still occupied by the Spanish. In fact, between 1739 and 1740, a group of Africans outside of Charleston along the Stono River, led by a brother named Cato or Jemmy, started on their way to Florida. This uprising has gone down in history as the "Stono Rebellion." Approximately 25 whites were killed "and with drums beating and flags flying, [they] set off for St. Augustine."

As Africans banned with indigenous Americans in the Sea Islands, many of them continuously fought against the Europeans. Eventually, the day came when the Europeans fought each other-the beginning of the Revolutionary War. In 1775, war appeared to be inevitable.

In 1770, after Crispus Attucks, took the first bullet, the lines were drawn for battle. This so-called "war of independence" was a means to "independence" for many enslaved Africans. Scores of Africans left the plantations and joined forces with the British to fight. There were over 5,000 soldiers of African descent as the war went on. They were promised grants of land and freedom for their bravery. Yet, like Gullah/Geechee folks say, "promisin' tak don cook rice."

Whether they banked on the promises and fought for the British or if they sided with the "Americans," many of the African men that joined in this war which was not their own, found freedom in death. St. Helena had its fair share of Gullah/Geechee casualties of this war. The British took possession of the islands in March 1780, but the battles that the islands were to see were not over.

As more people moved into "America" the population of the Sea Islands continued to rise as well. The numbers of African and indigenous American alliances grew also. This situation was not well received by European "settlers" who continued to usurp land from and fought and killed the indigenous people.

Since the importation of enslaved Africans into North America was forbidden as of 1808 when the United States of America implemented its support of the abolition of the British slave trade, the value of escaped Africans rose drastically. Slave catchers and bounty hunters began to regularly invade "Seminole" and "maroon" areas to capture and enslave Africans, Native Americans, and their offspring. This caused a great deal of unrest among the indigenous people. All this culminated in the First Seminole War.

On May 28, 1830, Andrew Jackson signed the Indian Removal Act which was the beginning of sending many indigenous people of the southeast away from their native lands. They went west on the "Trail of Tears." Although the sound of the Oconee, Apalachicola, Yamassee, Yuchi, Sawokli, Tamathli, Chialta, Eufaula, Calusa, Igbo, Senegalease, Ashanti, and Coromantee had not been heard in a while, the silence of the Seminoles at that time was only the calm before the storm. The continued degradation and annihilation of land and people was not to be tolerated by the Seminoles. Again they decided to strike back.

Many Europeans that opposed slavery saw this from a different viewpoint than the First Seminole War. In fact, "with some justification abolitionists charged that the Second Seminole War which broke out in 1835 was not really an Indian, but a Negro war, resulting from southern white determination to capture and enslave Negro-Seminoles."

St. Helena had a number of Africans and indigenous Americans involved in the Seminole Wars, especially the second one. Of course, the many Europeans that had now settled on St. Helena wanted to protect what they deemed as "their property." Thus, they too sent troops into the Seminole War. The *St. Helena Volunteers*, which had been described as a group of "irregulars," fought against the Seminoles as did others for seven years.

The following plantation owners were within the St. Helena's Parish as the plantation system grew even after these battles:

Enslaver	Plantation	Plantation
Dr. Francis Capers	Capers	Little Capers Island
Mrs. Eliza H. Jenkins	Chaplin	Indian Hill
Thomas Aston Coffin	Coffin Point	Frogmore, Cherry Hill
Rev. Stephen Elliott	Newbury	
Mrs. Patience W. B. Izard	Eustis	Tomotley
Edgar Fripp	Palmetto Hill	
John Fripp	Corner Farm	Homestead
William Fripp	Republican Hall	Point Place, Pine Grove
Dr. Thomas Fuller	Fuller	
Dr. William J. Jenkins	Jenkin	
Henry McKee	McKee	
John J. T. Pope	The Oaks	Feliciana
Richard Reynolds	Jerico	Lady's
Archibald Hamilton	Seabrook	Rest Park
John Joyner Smith	Blue Mud (Savannah River)	

As these Europeans sought to expand their plantation territories and increase their profits, there were always those working toward freedom. As abolition and industrialization grew throughout the north, a rift grew between Europeans there and the ones in the south. Yet, the Africans of St. Helena continued to grow closer together and to build a strong culture on a spiritual foundation while looking to God for the day that they would decide their own destiny.

Sing to the Spirit

To soothe the pains of the bodies worn out from the day in and day out hard work; and beaten and strained by the memories of separated families and distorted heritage; to focus on duties that needed to be carried out; to send coded messages of departure into "freedom"; to continue the stories of ancestors and noted events; to offer tributes; and most often, to lift up the Spirit, Gullah/Geechee Sea Islanders sang.

The songs they sang then are still echoed in the tides of the Atlantic and the marsh that surrounds St. Helena. On many peaceful, warm nights, you can hear the whippoorwill sing. Many Sea Islanders actually say that this bird talks. It is attributed with telling people to "Get a job!" or even "Get the president out the White House!"

If we could really understand this bird or communicate with the trees in which it perches. We would definitely know more about the days gone by. The days when the Gullah/Geechees praised the Creator under the rising sun and in the woods under the shine of the moon. The days when they relied upon and believed in herbs and the healing hands and wisdom of midwives and doctors such as Buzzard.

As ships came from Alkebulan bringing the most precious resource- human beings, these people brought centuries of science with them. The midwives of St. Helena knew pregnancy by sight and touch. They also knew what the medicinal qualities of various vegetation was. These women and other herbal doctors or healers would prescribe tonics for various maladies including menstruation cramps, morning sickness, or even lactation. Other "roots," teas, soups, extracts, and tinctures were used for day-to-day ailments and to keep the body strong.

One of the ships from the continent eventually brought over a man which came to be known as Dr. Buzzard. Just as the animal with whom he shared a name, he had cunning and patience. This statuesque man, who was always dressed "sharp" (often in white) and wore purple shades to shield his eyes, brought with him the knowledge and power of what has become a feared religion-vodun or voodoo.

As Dr. Buzzard practiced on St. Helena Island, he was not interfered with by his enslaver. It is difficult to say if this was out of respect for the fact that Dr. Buzzard did what his tasks were; because Dr. Buzzard "chewed the root" on him; or simply that the man was afraid of Dr. Buzzard. Whatever the reason, this doctor became known from plantation to plantation to plantation. Thus, many would steal away during the night to get to him and receive treatment for ailments and powders, potions, and mixtures to rid themselves of certain people and patterns. Some wanted to change or obtain "luck" and/or love.

As Dr. Buzzard gave them things to work on their bodies and emotions, he also worked on their minds. He let other islanders know that "ef hunnuh tink free, hunnuh be free!"

Freedom came for many through the upliftment of their spirits. A typical St. Helena way of achieving this is through songs. Many of these songs helped them work in the blazing sun day after day without pay and without gratitude or acknowledgement. The field songs keep them moving through it all, but the most powerful songs were the spirituals that emerged from the bush arbors and the praise houses.

> *"I heard the voice of Jesus say,*
>
> *Come unto me and rest.*
>
> *Lay down thy weary one, lay down*
>
> *Thy head upon my breast.*
>
> *I came to Jesus as I was weary, worn, and sad.*
>
> *I found in Him a resting place and he has made me glad."*

This hymn which is often sung now in "common meter" is a more formal presentation of the "call and response" that was carried on in the woods on plantations. These gatherings were opportunities to fellowship, share information, praise God, and shield departures or uprisings of some Africans. Europeans wanted to discourage meetings by masses of Africans especially "secret" ones, but they thought that praise was good. Of course, there still needed to controls on this praise, so eventually each plantation was allowed to have a building in which these meetings could be held. Thus, St. Helena had its "praise houses."

The Croft Praise House was built by Mr. Kit Chaplin. Paris Capers was one of the elders there.

These small whitewashed wooden buildings were always open and used for people to meet in and testify, pray, and uplift the Spirit in songs. Some praise houses were the homes of the oldest spiritual leaders on the plantations. They still stand in Coffin Point, Croft, and Jenkins. The voices from them carry for distances and ring out even in the ears of those who "bin da tun e back on da Lawd."

Although edifices now exist, the woods were not eliminated from the praise process. As a Gullah/Geechee became a "member" of a Christian congregation not only did one have to confess Jesus Christ as his or her Lord and Savior, but one had to be baptized.

Gullah/Geechees believe in hard work and truth. Therefore, this was carried into the Christian practices of St. Helena. You could not simply come forth and say, "I want to be baptized," and get taken to the water to become a part of the "body of Christ." You had to be sure that this was a "true choice."

Oh, it was always a night of celebration when someone came to the alter and yielded their will to the Lord. Someone would immediately "raise" a song:

> *"Jesus call you. Go een de wilderness.*
>
> *Go een de wilderness. Go een de wilderness.*
>
> *Jesus call you. Go een de wilderness.*
>
> *To wait upon de Lord.*
>
> *Go wait upon de Lord.*
>
> *Go wait upon de Lord.*
>
> *Go wait upon de Lord, my God.*
>
> *He take away de sins of de world/*
>
> *Jesus a-waitin'. Go een de wilderness.*
>
> *Go, &c.*
>
> *All dem chillun go een de wilderness*
>
> *To wait upon de Lord."*

This was not simply a song, but the directions for the next step in being "saved"-"seeking." The religious tradition known as "seeking" is not unique to St. Helena Island. It spans the entire Gullah/Geechee Nation and was one of the many aspects of cultural continuum that came to North America in the hulls of enslavement vessels. This tradition was easily fused into Christian worship given that Deuteronomy 4:29 in the Bible reads" "But if from thence thou shalt seek the Lord thy God, thou shalt find Him, if thou seek Him with all thy heart and with all thy soul."

The "seeking" process involves consistent isolation from idle talk and activities. The candidate for baptism is to meditate and pray in order to seek the message that God has for him or her. Parts of that message come in the form of visions or dreams that are listened to by the teacher or guide of the candidate. This person teachers the candidate the catechism and assist them with their study of the word of God. They make sure that they stay on the path that they have now freely chosen so that they can reach Jesus who freely gives.

On many nights on St. Helena whether it was winter, spring, summer, or fall, girls boys, women, and men could be found on their knees in the woods in the dark of night. These Gullah/Geechees were there to pray as a part of their "seeking" process. They had to go out for as many nights and for as many hours as it took for them to "find the Lord." They took to heart the scripture "And ye shall seek me, and find me, when ye shall search for me with all your heart."

As baptism grew near, consecration services were held in which testifying and praise continued. "De chu'ch" prayed for the "seekers" and sang---

"How did you feel when you come out the wilderness?

Come out the wilderness.

The response of:

"I felt like shoutin' when I come out the wilderness."

"I felt like singin' when I come out the wilderness."

"I felt like runnin' when I come out the wilderness."

were the closest verbal representation that the "saved" parties could come from to express their new life "leaning on the Lord." Yet, the energy and feeling that filled the praise houses and fills the churches and the members of the congregation were powerful and strengthening to St. Helena.

> ***"With my soul have I desired thee in the night; yea, with my spirit within me will I seek thee early: for when they judgements are in the earth, the inhabitants of the world will learn righteousness."***

The inhabitants of St. Helena continued to grow and to thrive. As the Gullah/Geechees procreated and multiplied, more and more Europeans also started coming to the island and some stayed. Their occupation led to the building of the first church buildings on the island. In 1740, the Chapel of Ease was built on one of the two original roads that ran through St. Helena Island. This road came to be called "Land's End Road" and it takes people to a historic plantation area that bears the same name.

The Chapel of Ease was built as a place of worship for the few "slave owning" families that first tried to live on St. Helena Island. In 1868, Methodist freedmen had used the building for a short period of time. The names of the enslavers that had dwelled on the island are etched within the burial markers at the location just outside this tabby structure that has simply been a ruin since a fire burned it down in 1886. The tabby structure is still a place that is frequented by those that seek knowledge of this aspect of architectural skills that the Africans and indigenous Americans had as well as by those that seek a scenic place for ceremonies and photographs.

Just as was the case with the Chapel of Ease, the labor and engineering skills of the enslaved Africans were used to build the Brick Baptist Church in 1833. This building was built with a balcony that was no doubt the area for enslaved people if they were to attend services with their enslavers. However, during the Civil War, the church became the worship center for freedmen while the Chapel of Ease was used by the missionaries, Anglo soldiers and teachers.

The spirit of the freedom and liberty that Gullah/Geechees knew was not only their Christian right, but also their human right. It was evoked in their songs during the period of enslavement when even places of worship were segregated, structured, and confining events. Therefore, the bush arbors and praise houses served to be any place where Gullah/Geechee gathered together and freely expressed themselves and their faith. At no point did they lose sight of God or their day when they would emerge from bondage.

"We'll soon be free,

We'll soon be free,

We'll soon be free,

When de Lord will call us home.

My brudder, how long,

My brudder, how long,

My brudder, how long,

'Fore we done sufferin' here?

It won't be long (Thrice.)

'Fore de Lord will call us home.

We'll walk de miry road. (Thrice.)

Where pleasure never dies.

We'll walk de golden street (Thrice.)

Where pleasure never dies.

My brudder, how long (Thrice.)

'Fore we done sufferin' here?

We'll soon be free (Thrice.)

When Jesus sets me free.

We'll fight for liberty (Thrice.)

When de Lord will call us home."

In 1861 as the colonists prepared for war again on what was now deemed "America's" soil, St. Helena continued to go on in its usual fashion. Gullah/Geechees gradually got the word about the disruption that was striking the south, but cotton still needed picking. As they sang, things heated up surrounding the Sea Isles. Yet, voices still rang out in harmony. The Spirit told them that freedom was near. Since the drum had been banned, the word spread through the rhythm of the voices...

"Stay een da field

Stay een da field

Stay een da field

'til the war has ended..."

At 9:25 on November 7 a war fleet approached the entrance of Port Royal Sound and "it was fired upon; and the bombardment began." (Rose 11) This was the beginning of what islanders now call "Big Shoot."

"The Confederate flags came down and evacuation began. The booming of the heavy gunfire rolling over the islands was the signal for flight and confusion. Negroes streamed in from the fields and found the white people hastily preparing for flight. "The Sea Island Negroes were, therefore, after November 7 neither slave nor free, but 'contraband' property, subject to seizure by the federal authorities."

As chaos developed on St. Helena with ransacking of property being done by islanders and soldiers and crops being burned by previous "owners" at night, Gullah/Geechees of St. Helena continued their day-to-day activities. In fact, just as other things were being restructured on the islands, several of the Gullah/Geechees who had formerly been seated in the balcony came down to the floor and the pulpit and took over *Brick Church* in 1862. The church had been abandoned just like other buildings that the Europeans had used on the island.

"On fine Sunday mornings throughout the spring, an astonishing array of dilapidated carriages could be seen winding over the dusty roads, converging on the 'Brick Church,' the Baptist fold on St. Helena Island. The unpretentious sanctuary was on these occasions filled to overflowing with Negro worshipers who occupied every available space-windows, doors, and aisles.

Those who found no place inside sat under the oaks in the church yard, leaning against the marble gravestones of masters truly departed forever. Susan Walker, given to romanticizing, saw such a tableau one Sunday and thought 'the Great Master must have arranged them' to illustrate that they were "God's images cut in ebony'."

While the Gullah/Geechees continued their plans to keep their souls to order, there were plans being made for their place in American society i.e. "the Union." A young Boston attorney named Edward L. Pierce was asked by Secretary Salmon P. Chase to go to Port Royal "to look into the contraband situation." Chase was an abolitionist that was part of the cabinet of President Abraham Lincoln. On February 3, 1862 Pierce sent a report to Chase in which he stated that although the Negroes "as yet in large numbers unprepared for the full privileges of 'citizens,' the islanders were to be managed 'with sole reference' to preparing them for such privileges." If the experiment of a guided transition to freedom could work in the Sea Islands, where slaves had lived in such great isolation and ignorance, Pierce thought it could be "hopefully attempted" anywhere in the south.

Pierce also met Mansfield French, a New York minister who came to Port Royal at the request of Lewis Tappan to see what the *American Missionary Society* could do for the slaves. French was an abolitionist friend of Chase who worked with the *American Missionary Association* to establish the nations's *Freedmen's Aid Society*.

Eventually word was sent north and New York and Boston groups of abolitionists, educators, and missionaries came together to begin to set up a strategy for the first phase of the "Port Royal Experiment"- education. On March 3, 1862, the Atlantic departed from Canal Street in New York City with various supplies and teachers aboard.

Upon arriving on St. Helena the Gideonite newcomers had to get accustomed to the Gullah/Geechees who made their inquiries about how much "lurnin" the women had and what their "fuss" names were. They began to open up for what was to become an interesting co-existence. The newcomers set up at "The Oaks" on St. Helena and began getting more acquainted with the Gullah/Geechees.

"The Oaks" house had just been built in 1855 for John Jeremiah Theus Pope and Mary Frampton Townsend Pope. Edward L. Pierce chose this location because it was the first to be reached by boat coming from Beaufort to St. Helena Island.

The *Pennsylvania Freedman's Aid Society*(or *Relief Association*) backed by Quakers was organized by James Miller McKim from Philadelphia and they were interested in having the missionaries that they sent down begin a process of educating the masses. Thus, in April 1862, the missionaries arrived and set out to establish a school. The educators found that there was an eagerness on the part of the people to learn to read and write. So, they now needed the students and financial support. There were several different efforts to have the work of those such efforts supported. Edward Philbrick tried to have contrabands become a paid work force to grow cotton. The money from the cotton sales was to be combined with donations from the *Freedmen's Aid Society* backers in the north in order to support the missionaries and the schools.

As Towne and Murray began the school in the back room of the house at "The Oaks" on St. Helena on June 18, 1862, they found it interesting that many people, especially drivers, knew how to read. *The Fundamental Slave Code of 1740* prohibited the teaching of writing and left reading to the discretion of individual masters. Also, additional laws had been attempt to further curtail reading being under taken by the enslaved. "Even reading, however, was proscribed in 1834, by servile insurrection and prompted specifically by a desire to put it out of the power of the slaves to read abolition protested the 1834 law on the ground that it was as necessary for a Negro Christian to read the Bible as for a white one, but they had never made their point with the legislature. Theoretically, by 1862 there should have been no former slaves in South Carolina able to write, and very few able to read."

Many Gullah/Geechees had learned writing due to their association with other enslaved people that had been associated with plantations owners and overseers' children. Many drivers would learn directly from their enslavers because this would be more beneficial to the enslaver. Yet, this was not the only way that the Gullah/Geechees learned. Gullah/Geechees also passed on information to and taught one another. There were certain "underground" schools that were run by "free Blacks" that also taught the enslaved. In fact, some St. Helena Gullah/Geechees were able to be taught by Jane DeVeaux who kept a school in Savannah, GA.

The Gideonite educators that came in from the north went out into the community to points as far away as Coffin Point (the well known Sea Island cotton plantation that was previously owned by Ebenezer Coffin who had been born in Boston in 1763) to enroll children and adults in classes. The first students were nine adults. The class eventually grew to 47 pupils or all ages and continued to increase. Thus, by September of 1862, a new building was needed. So, as Laura Matilda Towne, a "Gideonite" who was a representative of the *Philadelphia Port Royal Commission*, awaited this, she began to hold classes in *Brick Church*.

Ms. Towne and Ellen Murray)who had come to St. Helena from Milton, Massachusetts) developed *Penn School* which was the first normal industrial and agricultural school for the education of Blacks. Ms. Towne was born in Turkey to British missionary parents and was raised in Canada. Ms. Murray was raised in Salem, Massachusetts and later moved to Philadelphia. These two women came together after a speech Towne gave in Rhode Island to a Quaker community where Murray lived.

As Ms. Towne and Ms. Murray instructed the St. Helena islanders, up north, an African American woman struggled to join their mission. In 1837 this woman, Charlotte Forten was born and became another proud addition to a family of "free Blacks." Her father Robert Bridges Forten was the son of a wealthy and determined man, James Forten.

Charlotte's grandfather James was born to free Blacks in 1766 and was raised in Philadelphia. James was educated by abolitionist and later traveled, but returned home and became a sail maker's apprentice. "He became owner of the establishment twelve years later, and earned a fortune with the invention of a device to handle sails."

James' intense work in the abolition of slavery was undoubtedly passed on to his eight children. One that took special interest in it was Charlotte's father, Robert Bridges Forten.

Since Charlotte's mother passed away while she was very young, her father had her spend time at the homes of various family friends. Many of them were abolitionists. She was also educated by private tutors due to the fact that Philadelphia schools did not accept Black students.

Charlotte was eventually moved to Salem, Massachusetts where she graduated from *Salem Normal School* in July 1856. Charlotte went on to become a teacher and an ardent abolitionist despite the fact that she was weak due to failing health.

In August 1862, four years after resigning from teaching in order to rebuild her health, Charlotte visited, John Greenleaf Whittier in Boston. He advised her to apply to the *Boston Port Royal Educational Commission* for a job as a teacher. Charlotte waited months for a response only to be told that they were not sending women.

Charlotte pressed on and eventually applied to the *Philadelphia Commission* who accepted her application. "They set sail for Port Royal on October 27, 1862. John A. Hunn, who was an elderly Quaker, and his daughter, Lizzie, decided that they would go to St. Helena 'to open a store where Negroes could purchase goods at a reasonable price."

Upon arrival, Charlotte stayed in Oakland plantation and later moved closer to the school. Even though she was African American, she was not a "Geechee gal." Given this, she was not immediately accepted by the Gullah/Geechees, but she slowly made her way into the community and into the hearts of many of the St. Helena islanders.

The newcomers and Gullah/Geechees had many occasions to praise and celebrate together. One major celebration took place on January

1, 1863 when President Lincoln signed the Emancipation Proclamation. There was a special celebration at Camp Saxton just outside of Beaufort at which the proclamation was read, prayers were given, hymns were sang, and a great deal of food was partaken of.

On a day-to-day basis the process of Reconstruction was undertaken after this. Eventually, each plantation began to have their own schools and Ms. Towne was basically the superintendent over them. The school that many from the Frogmore Plantation call "Frogmore School" was the Towne-McDonald School. The school no longer stands, but the site of it has been secured as public open space and a sign denotes where it once stood.

The location of the schoolhouse at the boarder of Frogmore and the "Club Bridge" communities is just on the outside of the gates of "Frogmore Manor." This was the hub from which William Bull was able to successfully enslave from 100-170 Africans in order to operate a 3,300 acre Sea Island cotton plantation. The success of this "enterprise" is so well known that many people still call the entire St. Helena Island by the name "Frogmore" even though that is but one of the many communities that were formerly plantations on the island.

When Bull died in 1750, he willed the plantation to his son. In 1790, Frogmore became owned by Colonel John and Elizabeth Stapleton who most likely had the barn that still stands there built by the enslaved Africans. Later William Grayson became an owner and Thomas Coffin who also owned "Coffin Point" owned it when he died in 1865. The latter increased the number that he enslaved. Many of their descendants are the families that still occupy Frogmore and Hopes communities today.

Frogmore Manor still contains what has been called "the whipping tree" in which holes can still be seen from where the enslaved people were shackled to the tree for beatings. Archaeologist Ken Brown has worked on the grounds of Frogmore Manor and uncovered the areas that appeared to be the midwifes home and what he has written of as the "conjurer's cabin." Each of these places showed the

African continuum of the people within the ground and although the current "owner" does not want people to be aware of the existence of this facts that lie within the earth near the waterway, the ancestral spirits will always be there.

The spiritual energy of St. Helena can still be seen when even passing by the original location of the *Frogmore School*. The historic oak tree that stands proudly on the property seems to still shade youth playing in its yard even though children have not played there in many years.

In 1868, Laura Towne purchased Frogmore Manor for her and Ellen Murray. As she road her horse from there over the dirt roads from one school to the next, she would also check on different families and often help with complaints and health issues. She later even delivered messages and mail during her trips. Thus, she is often credited with being the first "post mistress" on the island. The boat that used to bring mail to the island would come in to Frogmore via the creek. Thus, the first post office on the island also had the name "Frogmore Post Office" and for years mail was sent to "Frogmore, SC." In the 1980s, chemist and school teacher, Joseph Sherman began a petition to insure that the correct name would be placed on the incoming postal building. At that time, the world finally started sending mail to "St. Helena Island, SC."

Even before the post office started and letters were sent to other parts of the world from the islands, people from different parts of the world continued to find this place and to make their way to the Sea Islands. Among the many women that came to the islands that make up Beaufort County, SC was Harriet Ross Tubman. Although she is famous for her work as a conductor and passenger on the Underground Railroad, she as also a nurse and scout during the Civll War and was stationed in Beaufort. She focused her work their on expeditions and assisting the previously enslaved Africans. She opened her own business that evolved into a cooperative with other women in Beaufort. She used this income to sustain herself instead of taking government funds for her service to the government.

1864 was a major turning point for St. Helena because in April of that year, the teachers on the island that had been obtained for them by the Commission. Three buildings were shipped and placed in a field opposite the church. This property had been "purchased from Hastings Gantt, a freedman who owned several properties in the area."

It took a year for *Penn School* to be built. The school got a bell six months later. The bell is located at the *Brick Church* now.

Charlotte Forten was not able to see the "experiment" to its completion. She left St. Helena Island in May 1864 in order to improve her health. She went back to Philadelphia and ended up marrying Reverend Francis Grimké there on December 19, 1878. She had one child, but the child passed away in 1880. Charlotte passed away in 1914 after many years of teaching, writing, and battling illness.

Ms. Towne and Ms. Murray continued to teach at *Penn School* for many years. Ms. Murray had arrived on St. Helena Island on June 8, 1862 and stayed until she died at The Oaks from yellow fever on January 15, 1908. Ms. Towne had preceded her when she died in 1900. They are both buried in the *Brick Church Cemetery*.

These women taught the St. Helena islanders the three Rs-"readin'," "'ritin', and "'rithmetic," but Gullah/Geechees taught them the spirit of a strong community and how to truly lift their voices in song.

"No more peck o' corn for me,

    No more, no more---

No more peck o' corn for me,

    Many thousands go.

No more drivers lash for me, (Twice.)

    No more, &c.

No more pint o' salt for me. (Twice.)

    No more, &c.

No more hundred lash for me. (Twice.)

    No more, &c.

No more mistress' call for me,

    No more, no more---

No more mistress' call for me,

    Many tousand go."

With the Power

Oh, none in all the world before

    We're ever as glad as we!

We're free on Carolina's shore,

    We're all at home and free.

Thou Friend and Helper of the poor,

    Who suffered for our sake,

To open every prison door,

    And every yoke to break!

Bend low Thy pitying face and mild,

    And help us sing and pray,

The hand that blessed the little child,

    Upon our foreheads lay.

We hear no more the driver's horn,

    No more the whip we fear.

This holy day that saw Thee born

    Was never half so dear.

The very oaks are greener clad,

    The waters brighter smile.

Oh, never shame a day so glad

    On sweet St. Helena's Isle.

We praise Thee in our songs today,

To thee in prayer we call.

Make swift the feet and straight the way

O freedom unto all.

Come once again, O blessed Lord!

Come walking on the sea!

And let the mainlands hear the word

That set the island free!

• Saint Helena Hymn by John Greenleaf Whittier

Due to several acts of Congress which levied direct taxes upon each state in the Union in order to raise war revenues and provide specific guidelines for the collection of these taxes, the Gullah/Geechee captives of St. Helena Island went from being "owned property" to "property owners." Surely, when the plantation owners abandoned St. Helena, they never thought that those who had worked St. Helena's soil would end up owning it and building on it for decades to come.

Since the "owners" of the land had abandoned St. Helena and the surrounding area, they were not around when it came time for the land to be auctioned due to non-payment of taxes. After much ado over whether or not the former enslaved should be allowed to bid and what price would be reasonable for the Gullah/Geechees, "On March 9, 1863, exactly one year after the arrival of the Gideonites at Beaufort the first land sales took place." 76,775 acres were put up for sale of which 16,479 was bought by individuals and the rest was allotted to the government.

The average price that individuals paid was $1 per acre. "Several plantations, about 2,000 acres of land, were purchased cooperatively by Negroes, who by pooling their small savings were able to preserve their right to live and work in their own places." This was the beginning of the "true" independence for St. Helena's Gullah/Geechees. "In November 1867, [Freedmen's Bureau Commissioner] Howard reported that 1,980 heads of families owned 19,040 acres of land in the Beaufort, South Carolina, Bureau subdistrict, having paid the government $31,000 for the property." "The value of personal property in St. Helena's Parish dropped from $5,271,050 in 1860 to a mere $106,635 by 1870. This reflected, or course, the lost value of the slaves and also the loss of personal property destroyed during the war."

The Anglo people calculated this loss in a number of ways without taking into account the self-worth of the Gullah/Geechees. Many European "businessmen" were amazed and disturbed by the fact that the islanders would not simply "work **for** them." Several Gullah/Geechees on different plantations decided to no longer invest in the increase of value or quality of life for others, but to do so for themselves. Thus, they would band together and raise their own crops. This allowed them to feed their families and they would sell a portion of the crops for profit. The money they made for was spent on clothing and staple goods that they could not grow or make. "The Civil War brought to St. Helena Parish a type of freedom different from that of most Negroes elsewhere, both then and in the future. Life in this part of South Carolina had a tangible element that Constitutional amendments could not provide: the beginnings of economic self-sufficiency."

> *"W'en war come, Missis tek me an two more n------, put we and chillun in two wagon and go to Bearnwell (Barnwell)....We stay in Barnwell all enduring (during) the war. My fadder had been de Rebel-been wid Mr. Marion Chaplin. W'en freedom come, Missie didn't say nutting. She jest cry. But she gib we uh wagon and we press (stole) a horse and us come back to St. Helena Islant. It tak tree day to git home. W'en we git home, we fine de rest ob de n----- yere been hab freedom four year befo we! I wuk for uh n----- name Peter White. Muh fadder came back, and buy 20 acre ob land and we*

all lib togedder. I gone to school one or two year, but I ain't lurn (learn) much. Four year after war, I buy fifteen acre ob land. Dat was dis yers same place w'ere I lib now."

Gullah/Geechees have maintained a level of self-sufficiency due to the fact that they have the greatest asset that anyone can obtain- richness of spirit and land. From the land they could feed themselves, their families, and their communities. To complement those who worked in the fields were those that worked in "een de crick." Men went out for the most part, but there were also women and girls that had the stamina to do the same work. They caught fish, crabs, shrimp, and other seafood and dug for oysters and clams. These items were brought back and cleaned, shucked and prepared for eating or preserving. Many island fishermen made money from selling their goods to the Union forces that lived at various forts in the St. Helena/Port Royal area.

Although the Union forces left Hilton Head Island Island, Land's End on St. Helena Island, and Port Royal Island during the first week of July in 1863, this was not the last encounter that Gullah/Geechees had with the troops. Fort Fremont was started at Land's End in 1898 as a protection during the Spanish-American War which ended before the fort was completed. This solid fort created of stone, concrete, and tabby was named after John Charles Fremont.

This site which was equipped with its own officer's quarters, barracks, and a brick hospital. From 1906 to 1910 the people at the fort were constantly under the threat of being moved out due to the fort being closed down. However, the Congress finally got around to coming up with more money to work on improvements and to send in more soldiers." The fort was decommissioned in 1930. The hospital building which was built in 1906 to replace a temporary building that had been there, became a private residence when it was sold that year at a public auction.

Just up the road from this fort is property that was purchased by forty-seven Gullah/Geechees that came together in 1920 and purchased what had been called the "Baker Plantation." In 1994 this 328 acres was turned into a non-profit organization which is now called "The Land's End Woodlands Club." The group made national news when a boundary dispute came about concerning 68 acres of the land which overlapped with what was purchased by media mogul, Ted Turner. The original plat had not been filed which did not allow clear title and boundaries to exist. Ultimately, the land in question was listed as having been given as a donation by Turner to the group so that the lawsuit could be settled and the media attention on the issue would die down. In 1996 the group got clear title.

Some Union soldiers and returning St. Helena Islanders made sure that they too had their own land. They did not rely on others to protect them nor to take care of them. However, they knew that they were entitled to being properly represented so that they would be able to continue the lifestyle that they had finally be able to obtain after the hardships that they had endured. So to that end, Gullah/Geechee Sea Islanders pridefully represented themselves at home on May 18, 1864 when they decided to make sure that they were represented nationally. At a rally in Beaufort, sixteen delegates were elected to go to the Republican National Convention. Four of the delegates were Black and included Prince Rivers and Civil War hero, Robert Smalls. For many years, Smalls stood his ground on the Congressional floor and spoke for his people. Given the outstanding legacy that he left, there is now a United Stated Naval vessel named in his honor.

Queen Quet and the Gullah/Geechee Nation Wisdom Circle Council of Elders pour the first libation for the *USAV MG Robert Smalls* when it makes it first voyage to Charleston, SC in the Gullah/Geechee Nation.

Gullah/Geechees stood to honor their own and to also take care of their own in the times of need. So, not only did they actively involve themselves in the political arena, they also started their own organizations. The *Pilgrim Lodge No. 1 of the Knights of Wise Men* was organized in Frogmore on St. Helena Island in 1870. It was organized as a fraternal order that would allow the members to have financial and farming support. This became one of the many "burial societies" that existed among people of African descent in the south. St. Helena had at least thirty of them at one point. They all came about between 1870 and 1930. *The Knights of Wise Men* had 350 members by its height in the 1920s.

The original *Knights of Wise Men Hall* was a wooden structure placed at the Corners Area in 1889. This is where meetings and community functions were held, especially for Emancipation Day, the 4th of July, Labor Day, and "Lodge Turning Out" day (when they recruited new members). Sometime in the 1940s, the concrete block building that currently stands next to the *Dr. Martin L. King Memorial Park* was built because there had been a fire that damaged the original structure. The *South Carolina Coastal Community Development Corporation* now owns this building and seeks to have a credit union eventually in the space. Across the street from this is the "Coop Store" building that is still owned and rented out by the descendants of members that owned shares within that organization.

With mass numbers of Gullah/Geechees owning large strips of farmland, they wanted to make sure that they could make the best of their new lives. Thus, they continued to be involved in the changes that were taking place and they also continued to educate themselves. Numerous schools were set up on different plantations.

This school at Coffin Point was one of the many that Rosenwald invested in.

However, field work often interfered with instruction. Many children, especially the oldest and most responsible ones in the family had to work in the fields before going to school, walk home after school, and then go in the field again. If the family had livestock, the care of the animals was also a part of this routine. Many children were also taken to the creek to check on the boats or to go out to harvest seafood.

Some students found it difficult to focus on their schoolwork because of the pressures of this schedule. Many got up when it was dark and did not finish chores until it was dark again. Thus, they would attempt to do homework by candlelight or lamp light which would strain their eyes and they would often fall asleep in their books from exhaustion.

After awhile, even some of the best students and those most anxious to learn had to leave school. They then worked at on the farm at home taking care of their families, selling their own goods, and/or had other jobs in different areas and at the homes of other people. While some went to different areas of the island and even off the island, more people started coming in. The first wave came when the Union troops approached Savannah, GA and more African people headed to the Sea Islands including St. Helena while Europeans again fled the area. Next people came in seeking the same education that was already known to those on St. Helena Island. Some of those that came were educated at the first, trade, agricultural and normal school for freedmen, *Penn School.*

Amongst the graduates of this institution that is now on the United States *National Register of Historic Places* as "Landmark Historic District," was York W. Bailey. York W. Bailey was St. Helena Island's first Gullah/Geechee medical doctor and the only one to have his practice on his home island. Bailey did his undergraduate studies at *Hampton Institute.* Upon receiving his degree there, he went on to graduate school at *Howard University Medical School* in Washington, DC and returned home in 1906.

Many St. Helena islanders have fond memories of Dr. Bailey. Dr. Bailey was born on St. Helena Island in 1881. He often was paid with livestock, eggs, etc. He would then take them to Beaufort and sell them for cash. He was the Treasurer of the *Knights of Wise Men* until he started losing his sight in the 1950s.

He had his home and practice in the "Corners" area on St. Helena. His home was ordered from a catalogue and shipped to Beaufort. He then had it brought to the island and assembled in 1915. This and the adjacent office are now on the United States *National Register of Historic Places*. Unfortunately, the office has not been maintained and may soon be lost due to weather damage. This is a painful sight to many that now pass by and recall the minimal fees that Dr. Bailey would charge for all the many types of illnesses and conditions that he tended to.

Dr. Bailey covered all things from colds to broken bones, major diseases to baby deliveries. For those who weren't well enough to make it to his office, they were seen at home. Dr. Bailey would arrive down the dusty roads with his black doctor's bag in hand and the right medicine "fa gee de sick one." That bag is currently displayed in the *York W. Bailey Museum* which was founded by the late Agnes Sherman at *Penn Center, Inc.* The museum started off in the Butler Building and is now in the Cope Building where shoe lasting was once taught. It was started after Dr. Bailey had passed away in 1971.

Laura Towne's spirit should have "taken kindly" to this happening since it is said that she practiced homeopathy also. This was one of the reasons that the islanders accepted her. They were accustomed to the practice since Dr. Buzzard also used a number of different types of herbs to heal ailing community members. Since the Dr. Buzzard passed away, there have been a succession of his sons and family that have continued the practice bearing his name. Thus, teaching the native practices of their people the next generations as is the Gullah/Geechee tradition.

Many of the Gullah/Geechee traditions were discouraged by the missionaries and teachers at the *Penn School*. As a result, most graduates of the school can no longer speak the Gullah/Geechee language even though they can understand it. They were ridiculed and often had corporal punishment issue if they were found speaking the language on the campus.

Penn School functioned as a school until 1948. During that year, the South Carolina Public School system was extended to St. Helena Island. Land was obtained by a native of the island the "St. Helena School" was built on what is now Highway 21. Although the school is now for lower levels, it at once was where St. Helena students went from kindergarten through 12 grade. With this new school in place, *Penn School* shared educated students until 1953 when its final senior class graduated.

As these graduates removed their tassels, a new life for them was beginning, but it was not simply because they graduated. As many of them went off the island to find jobs, join the military, and see the world, there were those that would come in to seek a place that would help reshape the face of America once again. The voices of a new movement would begin to ring out from under the oak trees as had happened almost one hundred years before.

Journey On...

The building of the Woods Memorial Bridge from Port Royal Island at Bay Street in Town of Beaufort across to Lady's Island in 1927 and then other small bridges such as Chowan Creek Bridge that connects Lady's Island to St. Helena that were built in the 1930s along with various causeways that became connections like the ones from Warsaw and Polowana Island to St. Helena, made arrival to the island much easier than it had been when boats were the only means of access. These bridges not only took Gullah/Geechees off the island, but brought others on. Ms. Cooley who was the principal at *Penn School*, warned Gullah/Geechees that if the bridge was built from Beaufort, the people would come on an try and take the land.

When Gullah/Geechee decided to journey off the island to work and to purchase things at stores along Bay Street in Beaufort, they were often met with disdain and discrimination that they did not feel when on the island. The bridge also brought people that started businesses in the Corners Community. The "Corner Store" was built by John Ross Macdonald who moved to the island from Rhode Island in order to improve his health. He partnered with George Wilkins and operated a firm that shipped Sea Island cotton from the island. The partners lived upstairs and would sell goods to the Gullah/Geechees from the store downstairs.

The post office occupied the building at one point before it got moved across the road to the "Waterhouse Store." In 1905 Mark D. Batchelder, who was a partner in the Macdonald-Wilkins and Company, came to occupy a new adjacent building. Joining him in the new office building was William Keyserling.

These businesses and others that followed on the islands were built by the support of the Gullah/Geechees that were customers there for generations. In spite of this, many of the store owners practiced discrimination. Some Gullah/Geechees would silently boycott them and others would speak out about their practices. Those that were willing to not only speak out, but to stand up against these practices soon became a formidable force in the Civil Rights Movement.

Many students and adults would go downtown Beaufort for marches and sit ins at restaurants. This came when the *Southern Christian Leadership Conference (SCLC)* started coming to St. Helena Island in 1963 for their annual meetings.

The meetings would take place in *Frissell Community House* which was designed by a New York architect and built by students of the *Penn School* in 1925 after Dr. Hollis Frissell of *Hampton Institute* began looking after the welfare of the school at the request of Ms. Towne. This facility had an auditorium, library, kitchen, and a dining room which made it convenient for all different types of community meetings to be held there. This building joined the Frissell Hall, Butler Building, Lathers Hall, a dining hall (now named for former Director Emory Campbell), Cope Building, Hose House, Pine Cottage, Retreat House, Darrah Hall, Orchard Cottage, Hampton House, Benezet, Arnet, Gantt Cottage, Jasmine Cottage, and Cedar Cottage. There was also a shed (now renovated and used for meetings) and a water tank on the campus.

SCLC implemented their "Citizenship Education Program" that taught adults to read in order to encourage the registration of Black voters and trained groups of prospective teachers under the direction of Dorothy Cotton and Septima Poinsett Clark. They then had their first meeting of *SCLC* affiliates there on March 12-13, 1964. This was a national meeting of fifty delegates from twelve southern states. They then returned in September 1965 for their first annual staff retreat. Dr. Martin L. King Jr. was with them at all of these events and at their 1966 staff retreat as well.

Some of the planning for the famous "March on Washington" occurred on St. Helena Island. As Dr. King and *SCLC* began to focus more on economics and poverty, they decided to strategically plan a direct confrontation with Capitol Hill regarding these matters. So, Monday, November 27 through Sunday, December 2, 1967, *SCLC* and Dr. King again had a retreat on the island. As they met that weekend and planned "The Poor People's Campaign," Dr. King did two speeches, "Why a Movement" and "the State of the Movement." Dr. King told them "I don't know if I'll see you before April, but I send you forth. Do something that will give new meaning to our own lives, and I hope, new meaning to the life of the nation. I may not see you before, but I'll meet you in Washington." These words may have been a premonition because Dr. King was assassinated on the 4th of April 1968 in Memphis, Tennessee. He did not physically make it with them to Washington that time, but his spirit was there when they arrived.

On the current grounds of *Penn Center, Inc.* is a retreat house named for Dr. King. He never got to stay in the building because it was completed one month after his assassination. As one listens to the wind traveling through the trees while walking the dirt road to get to the home, if you can tune in, you can hear the voices of Gullah/Geechee ancestors joined with Dr. King in repeating the words, "I will not be silent and I will be heard."

Over the generations, St. Helena Islanders have made sure that their voices were heard. Slavery, Reconstruction, Jim Crow, Civil Rights, and disco were all eras that took their toll on St. Helena. Yet, one can still hear songs of pride and renewal of spirit every Sunday morning as the doors of numerous Baptist and full gospel churches open their doors for worship.

I cum dis fa

Find no fault

Feel lik journee on...

This song and many others that have endured throughout the ages can be heard for miles outside of *Bethesda Christian Center, Ebenezer Baptist, Brick Baptist, Faith Memorial, Adam's Street, First African Baptist, Scottville, Orange Grove Baptist* and *Oaks True* and *Jehovah Church of Christ Holiness* churches. They can still be heard as Gullah/Geechees continue their daily work harvesting and planting and taking care of their yards and their families in the family compounds.

Those that had more helped others that did not have. Several people were able to begin businesses so that they could be self-employed and employ others. While just about everyone farmed something for themselves, most people also worked on the truck farms for large commercial farmers.

Jack Johnson and "Soldier" Washington from Orange Grove were two of the native farmers that would hire others to work for them. In later years, many Gullah/Geechees went from simply using bateau boats to using shrimp boats and owning docks. Some of these men included Pete Holmes, Harry Brown, Marvin Ladson, and Reverend Chisolm. One of the last men that can build these boats is Sam Moultrie, Sr. of Polowana Island while Captain Joseph Legree continues to keep up the cast net making just as the late Luke Smalls had done.

Local stores are located throughout the island. Some of these were started by Isaiah Chaplin, Sam Miller (*Seaside Mini-Mart* or *Miller Store*), "Buddy" Warren(*Folly Rd Grocery*). and *Frank Holmes* (Highway 21 Open Air Market). While these small stores made it easier for people to purchase an array of goods without having to make a trip all the way to "town," "E's Fabric" was a convenient location at which to purchase patterns and fabrics while also getting taxes done. Mr. Parker also runs the *ABC Package Store*.

Gullah/Geechees prefer the homestyle setting of these spaces where they can shop and talk over the larger chain stores and impersonal treatment. Thus, they still go to the homes of folks like Carolee Holmes Brown, Bertha Ladson, and Mary Holmes to purchase food freshly harvested from the field or put away in jars. These women are some of the few native islanders that still hold on to these traditions.

Gullah/Geechees also maintain the African American tradition of going to the hair salon or barbershop to get their hair done while hearing the latest news. Herman Smalls, Mr. Chaplin, Frank Capers, and Tecumseh Capers were some of the well known barbers from the island. Since their times, more and more Gullah/Geechees have gone into cosmetology and have opened store front locations after starting off in their own homes.

Many of the "cottage businesses" on the island are located in the same place that the "home based businesses" are-in the family compounds. Many people have had to fight to hold onto these family compounds because as people left the island, not only was a brain trust removed, but also a financial base. So, families started struggling to pay their land taxes and many have found themselves unable to. Also, as the bridges led people away from home, they brought in people that knew little or nothing about the culture who acted as agents of destruction to the family structure. They would tell the most intelligent students that there was nothing on the island. So, they should leave the area. They did their best to make sure that the students would not value the language that was their native tongue. As a result, many left and did not return unless they could not handle life in the bigger cities.

Those that did go to bigger cities would often come back assimilated into western cultural practices and no longer had an interest in many of the things that had built their communities and sustained them. They had forgotten about how the family and community worked together to keep them fed and often helped them obtain the money to go to college or to get on the bus that took them to the city for work.

As they left spaces void, alcohol and other drugs came in over the bridges and via the marinas that started to come up around St. Helena with gated areas being built on surrounding islands. Many wanted to move to the area for the feelings that brought them nostalgia about the "plantation era" and also to enjoy the "semi-tropical" environment. Orange Grove Plantation was one of the first places where someone built a "resort house." United States House of Representatives Member, Henry L. Bowles from Massachusetts bought the plantation from the Fripp Family and had the antebellum home demolished. He put up the present house in 1928 with a design that makes present day visitors believe it is an original plantation home. However, none of those exist on St. Helena Island.

This was an opening to how the "developers" or "destructioneers" would start to set their sites on St. Helena. As they did, the spirit of the songs and the spirit of taking a stand that St. Helena had been known for came back as well. Even the youths that had been moved into the space age and that wanted everything fast and looked for answers in television and computer screens instead of at the feet and aprons of their elders, were awakened and some started to get involved.

Those that took a stand brought about new facilities on the island to provide recreation and health care. *Scott Hall, Seaside Center*, and the *Leroy E. Brown Service Center* all came into being. The latter was named for the first Black to be elected to office in South Carolina since Reconstruction, Beaufort County Commissioner, Leroy Brown. He was the son of George Brown who taught basket making at *Penn School* in the 1930s and 1940s.

Marquetta L. Goodwine, who was "homegrown" on St. Helena Island, founded the *Gullah/Geechee Sea Island Coalition* after hosting the *"Ourstory & Heritage Conference"* on St. Helena Island in 1996. The Coalition opened "Hunnuh Home," as a research center that developed into the only archive in the world that is dedicated to Gullah/Geechee history, heritage, and culture. From this base of operation, Goodwine was able to connect with groups such as the *"St. Helena Citizen's Advisory Committee"* and the *"Lowcountry Alliance"* to continue to rally together groups that would fight against the incoming encroachment and lack of concern on behalf of the county.

The *Gullah/Geechee Sea Island Coalition* worked with the "Save Our Small Islands" group when the issue of building a bridge from small outlying islands to connect them to St. Helena Island came up just as they had worked with the aforementioned group. The groups successfully managed to stop the "development" of these islands that were less than 10 acres each in size. This started a consistent relationship between this organization and other coastal environment preservation groups.

Goodwine worked with numerous elders of the community to insure that the culture of St. Helena Island was not only considered, but protected as the county began a process of creating a Zoning District

Standard Ordinance (ZDSO) which was a requirement followed by their Comprehensive Plan having been adopted. Beaufort County responded to the voice of St. Helena Islanders that continued to go into Beaufort and fill up the county council chambers whenever they had a discussion concerning new laws that would affect the lifestyle of St. Helena. No such crowds have been seen on one issue affecting the island since the Civil Rights Movement. A new era had truly begun.

Goodwine became the chair of the *St. Helena Island Corners Community Preservation Committee* which was appointed by the *Beaufort County Council*. William McBride represented St. Helena Island on the council and Benjamin Johnson III represented the island on the *Beaufort County Planning Commission*. These two came together to work with a body of island residents that would then spend three years developing the "Corners Community Preservation Plan" which became Appendix K of the *Beaufort County ZDSO*. The Committee included the late Gloria Potts, the late Joe Stevens, Barry Augustin, Elizabeth Santagati, Kitty Green, Bernice Wright, the late Robert Middleton, Dean Hewitt, the late Edith Sumpter, and Reed Armstrong,

The community consensus on this plan was a precedent. Many people questioned how it was possible to get so many people that came from different viewpoints to agree on a plan for the economic development of this "priority investment district" called the "Corners Community Preservation District." The county has not yet invested the funding into the district that they voted would be invested. In fact, a parcel of property that has gone up for sale in the district has caused battles against major chain stores to take place as well. Still standing together, Gullah/Geechees were able to protect the island from this incoming tide of economics that would again benefit those that came in while simply taking from the support of those that are already on the island.

Just as the *Corners Community Preservation District Plan* drew to a close, the *South Carolina Department of Transportation* decided that they would come up with their own plans for St. Helena Island. They intended to bring in a five lane highway under the guise of "road improvements." Once again, the *Gullah/Geechee Sea Island Coalition, the St. Helena Corners Community Preservation District Committee*, the newly founded, *St. Helena Cultural Protection Overlay District Committee*, and the *South Carolina Coastal Community Development Corporation* came together and was supported by the *South Carolina Coastal Conservation League* in the battle to prevent the devastation by displacement that would come to St. Helena with such a massive highway coming through it. The community rallies that were held, radio program discussions, news articles, and national letter writing campaigns resulted in the *SCDOT* working directly with the *St. Helena Island Cultural Protection Overlay District Committee* that was then chaired by Marquetta L. Goodwine. The community received road improvements that fit the rural setting of the island without destroying the historic buildings in the Corners Community or removing homes and churches along Highway 21.

The *St. Helena Cultural Protection Overlay District Committee* was established by the *Beaufort County Council* as a result of the request from those who had served on the *Corners Community Preservation District Committee*. This group included Ivan Glover, Elizabeth Santagati, Bernice Wright, Anne Pollitzer, Jonathan Brown, Benjamin Glover, Karen Ward, Wesley C. Smalls, Chiquetta Coaxum, Rev. Simmons, Charlie Simmons, Agnes Holmes, Acie Johnson, and Marie Gadsen. In spite of a lack of support and opposition from Beaufort County representatives and staff, the group worked for more than four years to develop a plan that would actually provide a section of law that could be used by the Beaufort County Planning Department when building projects for St. Helena Island were brought in.

The group not only looked at issues on the island, but also in the environment that sustains the island. The proliferation of resorts and retirement communities has affected the traditional vocation of the local people. Runoff from poorly planned "development" has decimated South Carolina's shellfish beds-more than half are now closed. This has caused many of the Gullah/Geechees that have sustained themselves from the fishing industry to be in a position of hardship. Just as local trade in seafood has declined, so has the family farm which is central to the Gullah/Geechee people and their family compounds. The *CPO Committee* sought ways to reverse these trends.

As Hilton Head Island approaches build-out today, the Gullah/Geechee people on it have been marginalized and pushed to a corner of the island. The outcry concerning this led voters to the polls for a bond referendum to be initiated to support the county purchasing land and development rights from land owners in order to keep land in the county as "open space" and agricultural lands. The *Gullah/Geechee Sea Island Coalition* was again active in this movement. The referendum not only passed for the overall county of Beaufort, but the Town of Hilton Head Island was inspired to begin their own fund to also have such space on that island.

In the St. Helena Island voting district, three gated golf course plantations were placed on outer lying islands-Datha Island (renamed "Dataw" by those that did not realize the original spelling based on the Gullah pronunciation of this long existing community space), Harbor Island and Fripp Island through Planned Unit Development Zoning. The threat was a "clear and present danger" of the loss of the culture which was to be protected through the CPO District zoning that states:

> The Cultural Protection Overlay (CPO) District is established to provide opportunities to protect natural and/or cultural resources found on St. Helena Island. The Beaufort County Comprehensive Plan provides "actions" to be undertaken, which would prevent rural gentrification and displacement of residents. The intent of the CPO District is to protect St. Helena Island, its surrounding smaller islands, and the Gullah/Geechee culture herein from encroaching development pressures. Rapid in-migration would substantially alter the traditional social and cultural character of this area, as new residents represent different values and customs. The gentrification of the island would result in a greater demand for

urban services and eventually to the urbanization of the island. This can be particularly acute on St. Helena Island where maintaining the traditional lifestyle becomes cost prohibitive because of the value of land for development.

The CPO District acknowledges St Helena's historic cultural landscape and its importance as the center of the county's most notable concentration of Gullah/Geechee culture.

In November of 2002, the *Cultural Protection Overlay District (CPO) Committee* brought forth suggestions to Beaufort County. The *Beaufort County Planning Commission* acknowledged the group in June 2003 and the *Beaufort County Council* commissioned the group in August 2003. They immediately got to work on constructing a plan to:

Preserve traditional land use patterns; and
Retain established customs and rural way of life.

Thus, the CPO District Plan seeks to provide additional zoning and development standards based on meeting the following criteria:

- The omnipresence of an ethnic heritage
- Historic structures, settlements, and land use patterns
- Archeological sites
- Significant cultural features and sites

The CPO District encompasses the island of St Helena and is an overlay over the base zoning. The Gullah/Geechee culture and its physical setting on St. Helena Island is a treasure of national and international significance. As one of Beaufort County's last substantially rural Sea Islands and as the center of its most notable concentration of Gullah/Geechee culture, St. Helena Island requires additional levels of development standards to protect this important resource. Thus, the Cultural Protection Overlay Plan is to:

- Acknowledge St. Helena Island's Gullah/Geechee culture,

- Define St. Helena Island as a significant traditional cultural landscape,
- Assess the contribution of the Gullah/Geechee culture, and
- Develop specific provisions within the plan that will result in effective long-term protection for and continued existence of the Gullah/Geechee culture.

The Cultural Protection Overlay Committee unanimously agreed to take an active part in carrying out the policies of the Beaufort County Comprehensive Plan to:

"1. maintain the distinction between rural and developing areas with the County"
St. Helena Island is a rural area in which development that adheres to the traditional Gullah/Geechee living patterns is to be allowed, but also controlled.

"2. protect the character and quality of existing communities and ensure that new development shares the characteristics of diversity and quality of life that make Beaufort County unique"
The most unique aspect of Beaufort County is the existence of the Gullah/Geechee culture that exist here and all that has been created as a result of that cultures evolution in this land. Thus, the CPOs major duty is to protect the Gullah/Geechee community of St. Helena Island.

"3. define and perpetuate an ethic of quality growth"
The St. Helena Island Plan is a full definition of what the people of St. Helena Island seek in order to make sure that their growth is of quality.

"4. foster and manage economic development"
The *CPO Committee* seeks to work directly with the *South Carolina Coastal Community Development Corporation* and other state, federal, and international agencies to seek out economic development mechanisms and utilize them for community sustainability for St. Helena Island.

"5. manage growth through infrastructure investment policies and plans"

The *CPO Committee* has already begun to plan community workshops in order to gain more information on such options and will continue to seek things that will allow the infrastructure of St. Helena to be maintained in harmony with its rural character.

"6. recognizing and accommodating constraints to growth"

The *CPO Committee* seeks to always seek community input regarding the type of growth that is desired by the people of St. Helena Island. The major focus will always be with keeping in mind protecting the Gullah/Geechee culture of the island. All these things must be done also within the context of what the "Community Character" section of the Comprehensive Plan states:

"...it is important to integrate new development into the County in a way that will protect the aspects of the County that people value, including:
- *the quality of the waterways and therefore the health and continued existence of fish spawning areas, shellfish beds and shrimp;*
- *the quality of the natural environment;*
- *the history of the County evident in the landscape and scenic quality of the rural communities and towns;*
- *the stability of communities and the retention of land by the residents; and*
- *the diversity of the communities in terms of age, income and race.*

Cultural survival has shaped the debate on the most pressing issues affecting St. Helena Island and has helped to raise awareness to new level of local, national, and international attention and action. In 1998, Marquetta L. Goodwine and the *Gullah/Geechee Sea Island Coalition* approached Congressman James Clyburn with the concept of seeking to create legislation that would assist in protecting the Sea Islands from the continued encroachment. Congressman Clyburn had begun the process to create the "South Carolina National Heritage Corridor." So, he thought that initiating a process that would allow the *National Park Service* to determine how this could be done would be something that he would undertake.

In 1999, Congressman Clyburn took the legislation before Congress and was not immediately met with support. The *Gullah/Geechee Sea Island Coalition* continued to make national contacts in order to get a ground swell of support for this legislation. *Penn Center, Inc.* and other organizations started to join in the effort. However, Congress still would not initiate the process.

On April 1, 1999, Marquetta L. Goodwine went to Genevé, Switzerland to speak before the *United Nations Human Rights Commission* concerning not just the plight of St. Helena Island, but that of the Gullah/Geechee people. She became the first Gullah/Geechee person to speak on behalf of her people before the United Nations. After returning to a great deal of media attention to what had just taken place, Goodwine was called and informed that the legislation was finally moving in the United States Congress.

At the very end of the session in 1999, the United States Congress passed an act that directed the *Secretary of the Department of the Interior* to begin a study concerning the "Gullah people." In April 2000, The *National Park Service* announced a series of public meetings as a part of a congressionally authorized study of ways to preserve the Gullah/Geechee culture. The *Lowcountry Gullah Special Resource Study* focused on various contributions of the Gullah/Geechee people during the 18th and 19th centuries and "explored all aspects of this unique group that became such an important part of our nation's history." The first meeting was held at *Emmanual AME Church* in Charleston, SC and the *Gullah/Geechee Sea Island Coalition* worked to advertise and document this meeting. They hosted the second meeting at *Penn Center, Inc.* on St. Helena Island and then assisted with the five meetings held thereafter in areas in SC, GA, and FL.

On July 2, 2000, Marquetta L. Goodwine was enstooled as "Queen Quet, Chieftess and Head-of-State" 102 for the Gullah/Geechee Nation in a special ceremony that was held at Sullivan's Island in Charleston County, SC. This was the culmination of a year long voting process to establish the Gullah/Geechees as not just a people, but a nation and to elect the first leader of the nation. Numerous people from St. Helena Island was in the crowd of thousands that gathered for the event.

While the Gullah/Geechee Nation began its development, the *United States National Park Study* undertook its study. As a result of the study, United States federal recognition and recommendation of preservation of this culture, the *Gullah/Geechee Cultural Heritage Act* was legislated and passed by the US Congress in 2006. When it was signed into law by President George W. Bush, a series of new meetings were held for nominations to a United States Federal Commission that would now create the plan for a "Gullah/Geechee Cultural Heritage Corridor" that would run through the Gullah/Geechee Nation.

The corridor is one of 37 national heritage areas (NHAs) that exist in the United States. It is the only one that focuses on the culture of a group of people of African descent in North America. Two St. Helena Islanders, Queen Quet Marquetta L. Goodwine, who was chosen as an "expert commissioner for South Carolina," and Ron Daise were chosen as commissioners. Queen Quet is the chair of the General Management Plan Working Group and the Implementation Committee Chair for the Commission.

Even as the Commission continues its work, families on St. Helena Island find themselves having to take stands against not only "developers," but individuals that have moved onto the island and seek to destroy sacred spaces. Lawsuits have been taken to protect graveyards, cemeteries, and burial areas in Wallace, Dr. White/Edding White and Hopes Communities. The Hopes Community's first case was against a person that wanted to extract sand from next to a historic Gullah/Geechee burial area in order to sell the sand. This brought the islanders out in mass to *St. Helena Elementary School* cafeteria to raise their voices before the *South Carolina Department of Health and Environmental Control. (SC DHEC)*

That meeting was not the first encounter between *DHEC* and the islanders. In fact, many worked along with the *South Carolina Coastal Conservation League* and the *Gullah/Geechee Sea Island Coalition* to get the laws for bridge permits changed for the entire state of South Carolina. No doubt this will stem off some of the access and as a result, some of the devastation that comes when the bridges bring in more people that do not respect this unique and powerful culture that is nestled beneath the oak trees of this historic and environmentally sensitive island and its sister islands.

No matter what the future brings, St. Helena still has a heart that seems to beat ever so quietly on a regular day, but that raises to the sound of the drum that calls out to the people when she is in trouble. May her drums turn back into those of continued celebration and may they draw you there to be embraced by the beauty of this place on which you are comforted by the breeze that comes in from the surrounding seas. After taking in its history, just stop for a moment and feel St. Helena's serenity.

The Spirits walk St. Helena through the former homes of the Fripps.

The journey to this island is one of peace and healing unlike regular trips.

The highways and dirt roads reach out to Dr. and Edding White.

The elders are always around to tell the others what is right.

Here "Hopes" is a place and a feeling that's kept alive.

As people journey from McTuereous to Capers through Club Bridge, Cuffy, and Indian Hill.

They cross the same roads as their ancestors and make stops in communities such as Saxonville.

Oakland and the Oaks still hold their historical connections to Penn.

All of this combined is reason to journey to this place time and time again.

The Groves, Corner, and Frogmore

are only short drives to Warsaw and Coosaw.

One overlooks the marsh at Fripp and Edding Points

And one can hear people swing at the local "juke joints."

By the time you've really seen the island including "Land's End,"

I'm sure that you would have definitely made a friend.

As you walk, simply take an ancestors hand,

Then relax and take in the serenity of St. Helena Island.

Epilogue

The points on the journey of "slave ships" which linked to make the final side of the "slave trade triangle" included Cuba, Bermuda, and the Bahamas where the final exchange of humans for items took place.

African people especially Gullahs expanded their journeys as they broke the chains and became "maroon," "Seminoles," "loyalists," soldiers, and pioneers. They now cover the land and have enriched the world through language, art, cuisine, and many other things, but especially through the Spirit.

We will journey to those other places in the books to come.

Peace and blessings as you journey until our paths come together again.

Epilogue 2008

I am proud to say that this photo is still valid today. 13 years after the first edition of this book. Not just because I look the same, but also because Edding Landing still looks this way. We can also still safely go out into our waterways that surround St. Helena Island. In the midst of standing for and with my people there, there have been many along the way that have had negative things to say, but to that end, I add "If God be for us, who can be against us?"

I am thankful to all the people of my community and my family that have stood with me over what is about to be thirty years of continued efforts to protect my home and to protect my people. I truly love each and everyone of you or I would sit down like many do. I am sure that God and the ancestors would not let me rest if I did that either. So, I will keep on standing with you.

Given what I have lived to see come to pass, I KNOW that God is for us. Mi prey fa hunnuh chillun wha ain yet cum een wid wi. Tenk Gawd fa not be lik man an fa disya serentee.

• *Queen Quet*

Bibliography

Alleyne, Warren & Henry Fraser. The Barbados-Carolina Connection. London and Basingstoke: Macmillan Publishers Ltd., 1988.

American Heritage Book of Indians with narrative by William Brandon, 1961. rpt. New York. American Heritage/Wings Books, 1993 edition.

Cimbala, Paul A. The Freedmen's Bureau: Reconstructing the American South after the Civil War. Malabar, FL: Krieger Publishing Company, 2005.

Goodwine Family Reunion Journal 1987 compiled by Mary Goodwine Johnson.

Higginson, Thomas Wentworth. Army Life in Black Regiment 1869, rpt. New York: W. W. Norton & Company, Inc.

Jones-Jackson, Patricia. When Roots Die: Endangered Traditions in the Sea Islands. Georgia University of Georgia Press, 1987.

Neill, Wilfred T. Florida's Seminole Indians. Florida: Outdoors Publishing Company, 1956.

Power, J. Tracy. Topics in African American History 2: I Will Not Be Silent and I Will Be Heard: Martin L. King Jr, the Southern Christian Leadership Conference, and Penn Center 1964-1967. South Carolina: South Carolina Department of Archives & History, 1993.

Rose, Willie Lee. Rehearsal for Reconstruction: The Port Royal Experiment. New York: William Morrow and Company, Inc. 1986.

Rosengarten, Theodore. Tombee: Portrait of a Cotton Planter. New York: William Morrow and Company, Inc., 1986.

Wright, J. Leitch, Jr. The Only Land They Knew. New York. The

Free Press, 1981.

Wright, Robert Hughes. A Tribute to Charlotte Forten. Michigan: Charro Book Company, 1993.

Made in the USA
Charleston, SC
19 February 2015